Special Symbols:

This book is organized to guide the individual through the training. In addition to the Notes section there are a number of symbols used to help the participant throughout the presentation and workshop. For your convenience these symbols are repeated at the introduction of each section of this workbook.

Suggestion:

This symbol represents a suggestion or is a general statement relating to facilitation of the training.

Tip:

This symbol represents a tip to the Facilitator and is specific to the concept that the Facilitator is presenting.

Question:

This symbol represents a question that may be asked to the Facilitator or to the participants in the workshop. It is intended to foster interaction during the training.

Table of Contents

Introduction

Introduction 1

Section 1

5S Supply Chain & Logistics 5

Section 2

5S and Organization 23

Section 3

5S and Teamwork 43

Appendix

Appendix 57

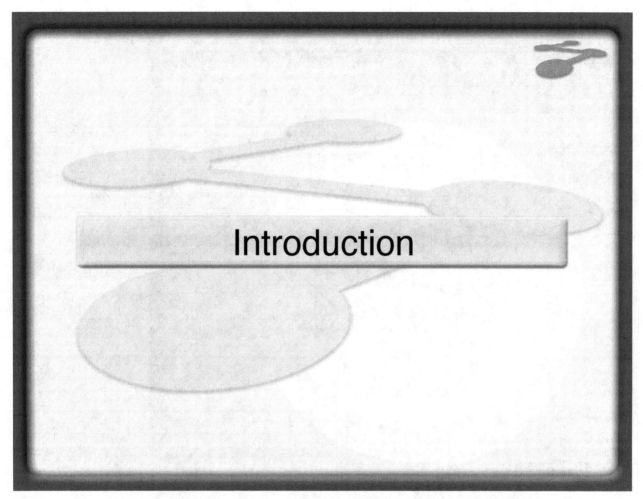

Introduction

Participant Workbook

In this Section

- Learn the 5Ss
- Introduction to the workshop layout

Participant Workbook Provided To:

_____

 Suggestion   **Tip**   **Question**

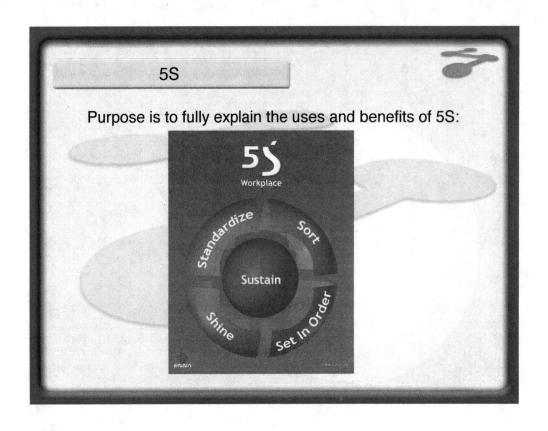

Notes, Slide 1:

_____

_____

_____

_____

_____

_____

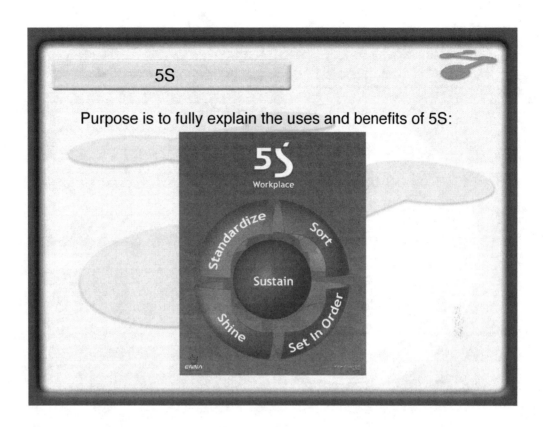

Notes, Slide 1 continued:

_____

_____

_____

_____

_____

_____

Tip:

Pay particular attention to the Facilitator when learning about a clean operation.

Question:

What do people generally think of an operation that is clean?

_____

_____

_____

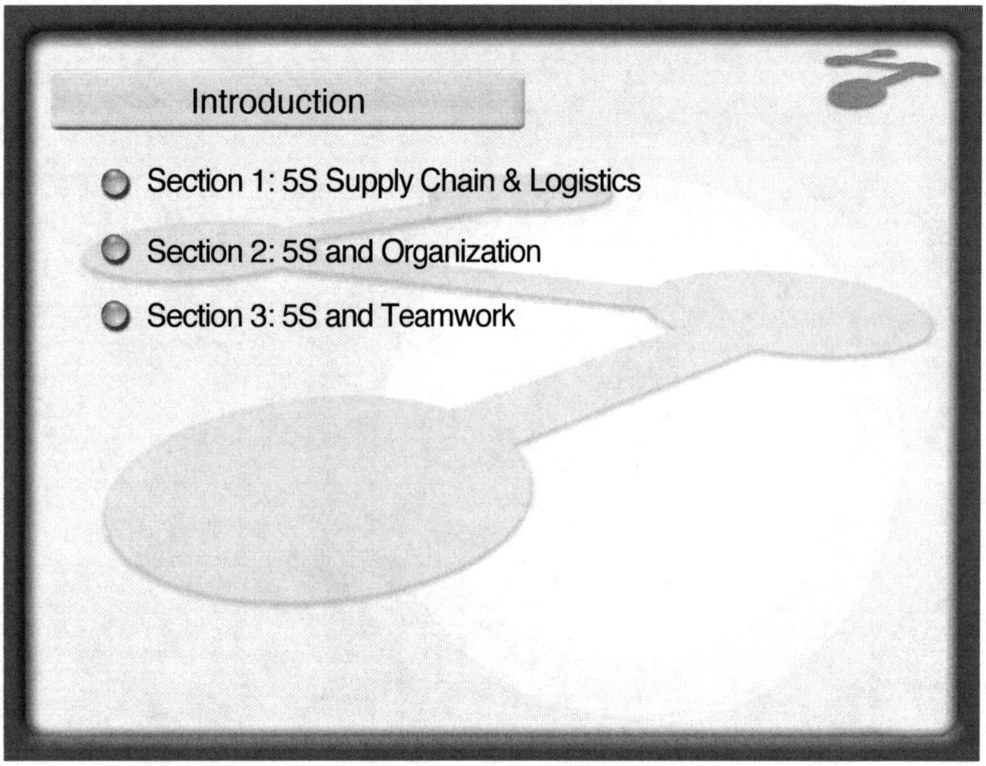

Introduction

- Section 1: 5S Supply Chain & Logistics
- Section 2: 5S and Organization
- Section 3: 5S and Teamwork

Notes, Slide 2:

_____

_____

_____

_____

_____

5S Supply Chain & Logistics

Participant Workbook

In this Section

- Learn the context of 5S
- Discover how 5S fits into improvement projects
- Study the 8 Wastes of Lean

The purpose of this section is to establish the underlying themes and principles of 5S. This includes not only providing the content and perspective for improvement, but also recognizing its value to both the participants and the organization as a whole.

 Suggestion   **Tip**   **Question**

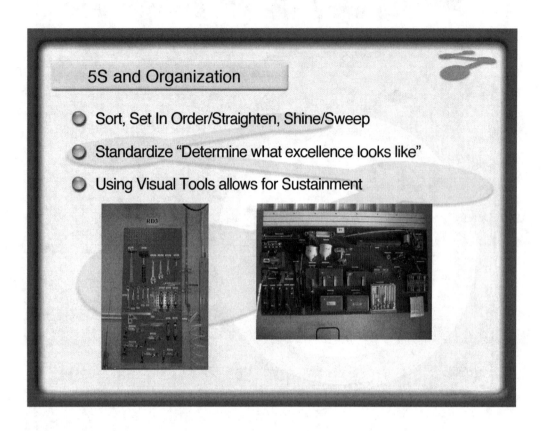

Notes, Slide 4:

_____

_____

_____

_____

_____

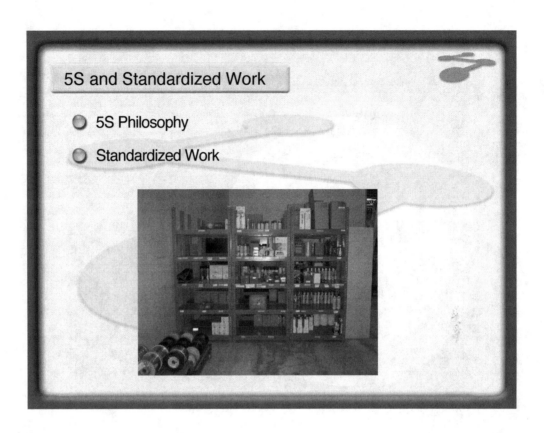

Notes, Slide 5:

_____

_____

_____

_____

_____

_____

Question:

Can you think of any kind of job that may require the need to be visual?

_____

_____

_____

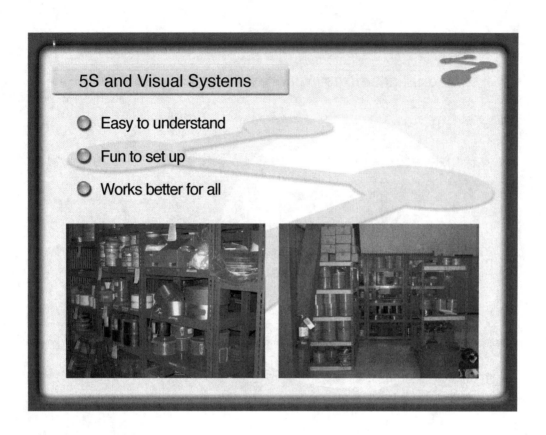

Notes, Slide 6:

_____

_____

_____

_____

_____

_____

Question:

Why are we doing 5S?

_____

_____

_____

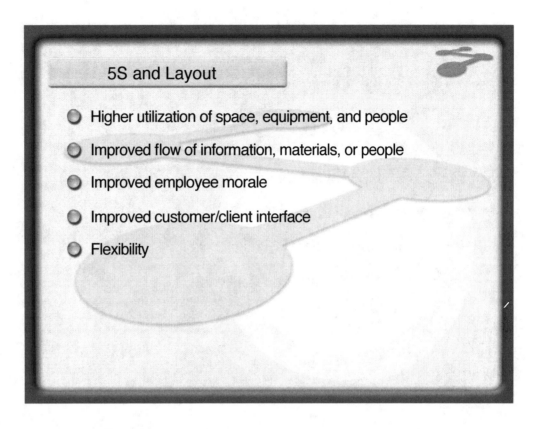

5S and Layout

- Higher utilization of space, equipment, and people
- Improved flow of information, materials, or people
- Improved employee morale
- Improved customer/client interface
- Flexibility

Notes, Slide 7:

Tip:
Focus on the 8 Wastes and what the definitions are.

Why 5S

- Allows us to maintain a more organized area
- Able to clean less and clean easier
- Makes our work area more productive
  - Makes the 8 Wastes obvious
  - Creates a standard for improvement
  - A way to get many people involved
  - Low real cost, high-impact for company

Notes, Slide 8:

_____

_____

_____

_____

_____

_____

Tip:

The 8 Wastes are a fundamental building block of 5S. Ask the facilitator to fully explain the wastes so that you understand them completely.

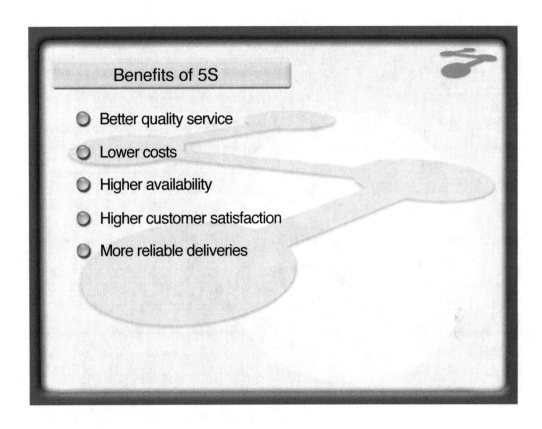

Notes, Slide 9:

_____

_____

_____

_____

_____

_____

Tip:

Operations should look at ways to only produce what is truly needed. Anything more will result in loss of efficiency and effectiveness.

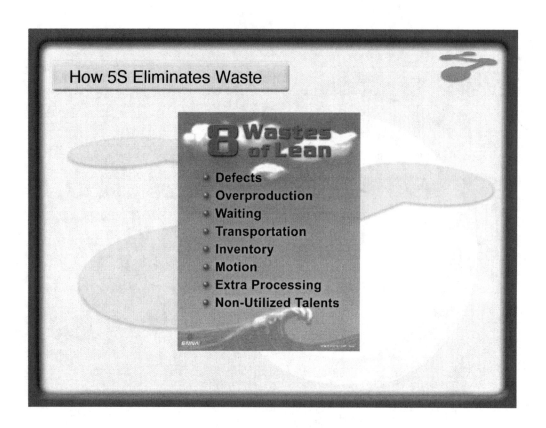

Notes, Slide 10:

_____

_____

_____

_____

_____

_____

Tip:

This is the hardest waste to find. However, the solution is simple. If you think about it, if it is truly a waste of over processing, then the ultimate solution is to find a way to not do it.

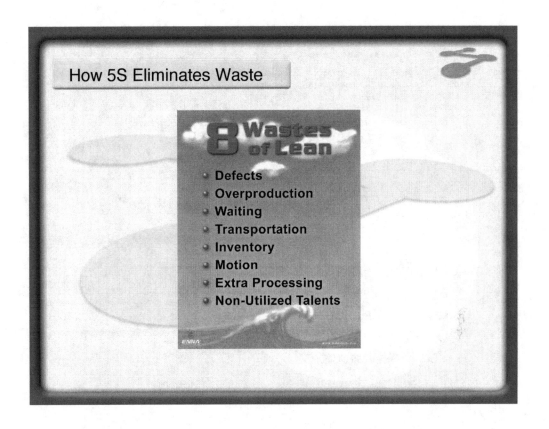

Notes, Slide 10 continued:

_____

_____

_____

_____

_____

_____

Defects/Rejects

Making bad parts, having scrap, wrong information, and/or having to rework items

Possible Causes:
- Batch Processing
- Quality of Materials
- Questionable Product Design
- Poor Work Instructions

Notes, Slide 11:

_____

_____

_____

_____

Waste Definition: _____

_____

Additional Example: _____

_____

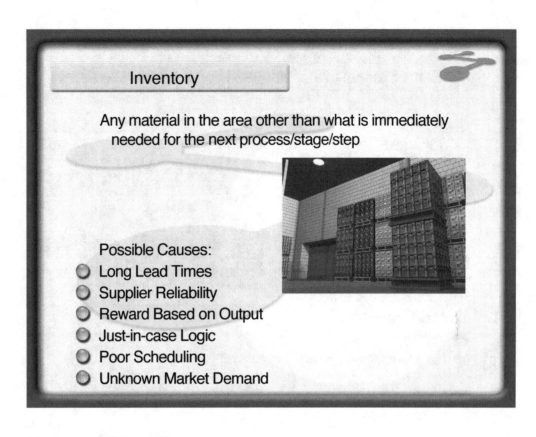

Notes, Slide 12:

_____

_____

_____

_____

_____

Waste Definition: _____

_____

Additional Example: _____

_____

Question:

What are the three stages that inventory lives as in your company?

_____

_____

_____

Extra Processing

Activity that adds no value to the product or service from the viewpoint of the internal/external customer

Possible Causes:
- Too Much Paperwork
- No Communication
- Too Many Steps
- Next Customer's Needs Not Known

Notes, Slide 13:

_____

_____

_____

_____

Waste Definition: _____

_____

Additional Example: _____

_____

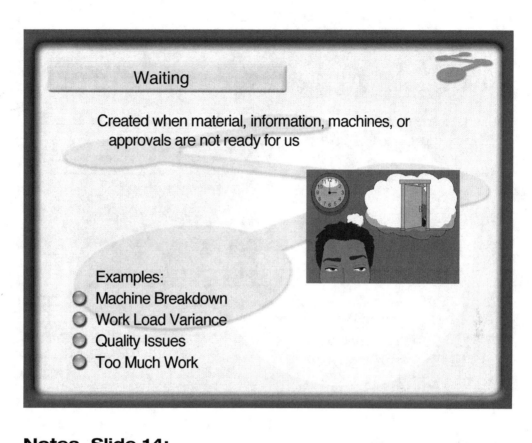

Notes, Slide 14:

_____

_____

_____

_____

Waste Definition: _____

_____

Additional Example: _____

_____

Question:

What are some times that you have waited? What are you waiting for?

_____

_____

_____

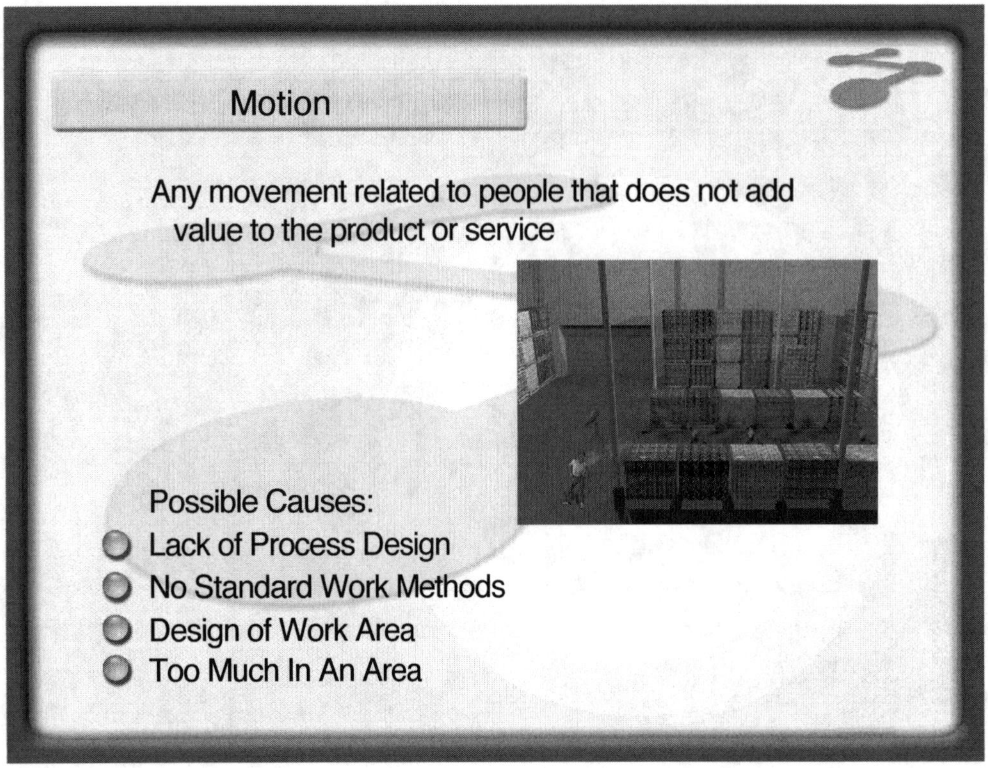

Notes, Slide 15:

Waste Definition:

Additional Example:

Transportation

Moving material from one area to another area in the company

Possible Causes:
- Batch Production Systems
- WIP Storage
- Layout of the Facility
- Staging Stock
- Utilization of Forklifts

Notes, Slide 16:

_____

_____

_____

_____

Waste Definition: _____

_____

Additional Example: _____

_____

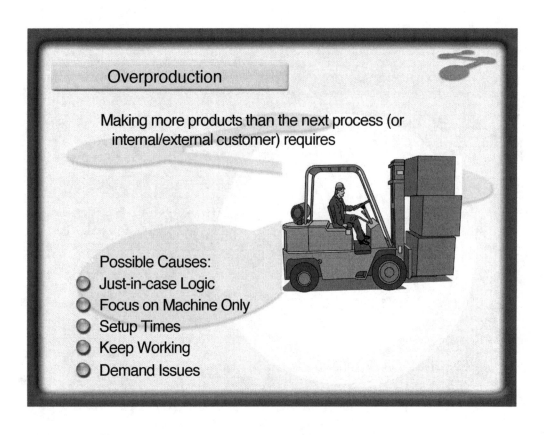

Overproduction

Making more products than the next process (or internal/external customer) requires

Possible Causes:
- Just-in-case Logic
- Focus on Machine Only
- Setup Times
- Keep Working
- Demand Issues

Notes, Slide 17:

_____

_____

_____

_____

Waste Definition: _____

_____

Additional Example: _____

_____

Question:

Why is overproduction so detrimental to an organization?

_____

_____

_____

Non-Utilized Talent

Not listening to or asking for employee feedback, lack of management support, and other cultural related issues

Possible Causes:
- Not Cross Training
- Lack of Management Support
- Not Wanting to 'Rock the Boat'
- Not providing assistance to workers who are actively seeking to improve the flow in their area

Notes, Slide 18:

_____

_____

_____

_____

Waste Definition: _____

_____

Additional Example: _____

_____

5S and Lean Operations

When organizing a warehouse, keep these things in mind:

- Space utilization of aisles and racks
- Most frequently used products should be closest to the shipping dock
- Visual management should be everywhere
- Create organizational checklists and job instructions to improve efficiency by ensuring future workers will understand processes
- Involve everyone in the creation of standard work

Remember, continuous review and auditing will help ensure continuous sustainment of 5S Standards.

Notes, Slide 19:

_____

_____

_____

_____

Waste Definition: _____

_____

Additional Example: _____

_____

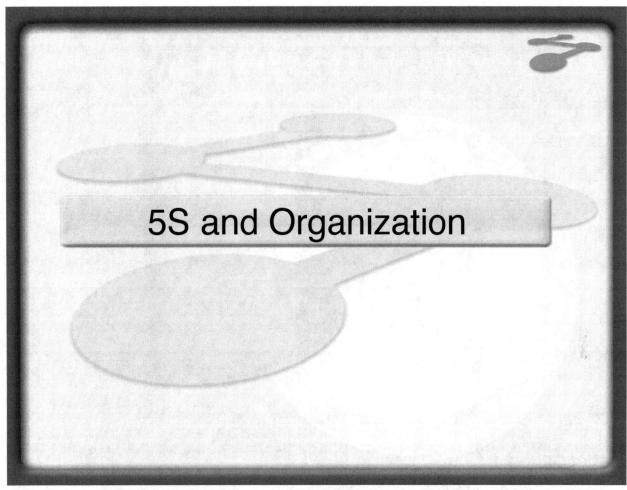

5S and Organization

Participant Workbook

In this Section

- The meaning behind 5S
- Procedures to employ when applying 5S to Supply Chain & Logistics functions
- The five elements of 5S
- Guide through the proper sequence of instructing 5S

When starting a 5S program it is important to focus on the right "S" at the appropriate time. In this next section we take you through the most logical flow to follow when facilitating 5S in your organization.

 Suggestion   **Tip**   **Question**

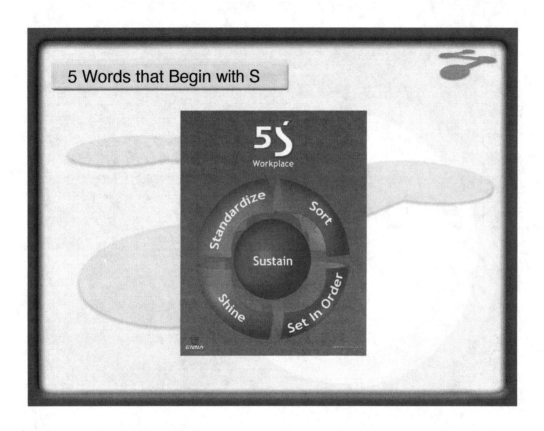

Notes, Slide 21:

_____

_____

_____

_____

_____

Question:

Why are we doing 5S?

_____

_____

_____

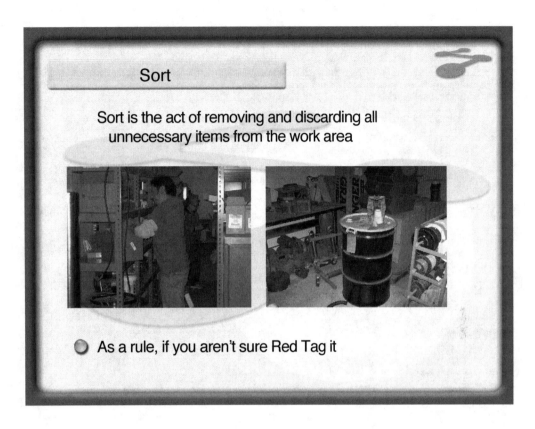

Sort

Sort is the act of removing and discarding all unnecessary items from the work area

As a rule, if you aren't sure Red Tag it

Notes, Slide 22:

_____

_____

_____

_____

Tip:

When sorting, make two categories:
1) what is needed for the job, and
2) everything else.

Sort Action Defined: _____

_____

Additional Example: _____

_____

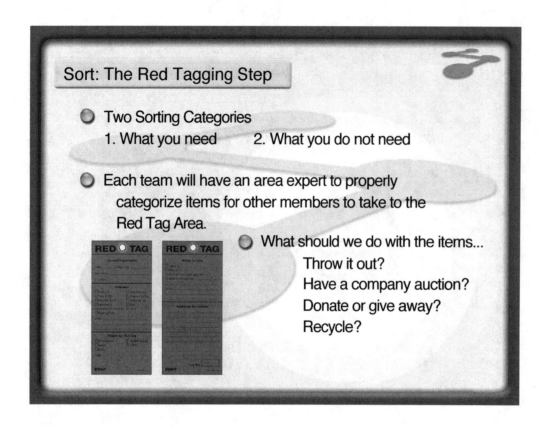

Notes, Slide 23:

_____

_____

_____

_____

_____

_____

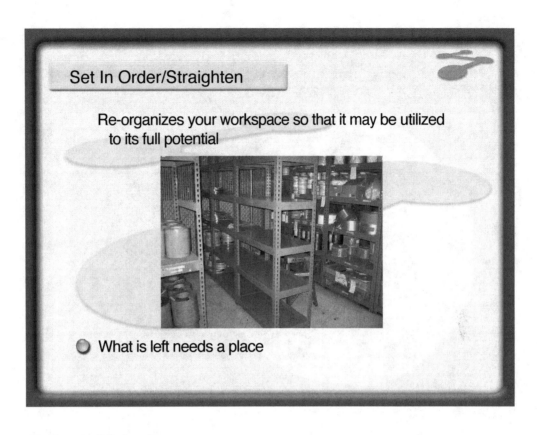

Set In Order/Straighten

Re-organizes your workspace so that it may be utilized to its full potential

What is left needs a place

Notes, Slide 24:

_____

_____

_____

_____

Set In Order Action Defined: _____

_____

Additional Example: _____

_____

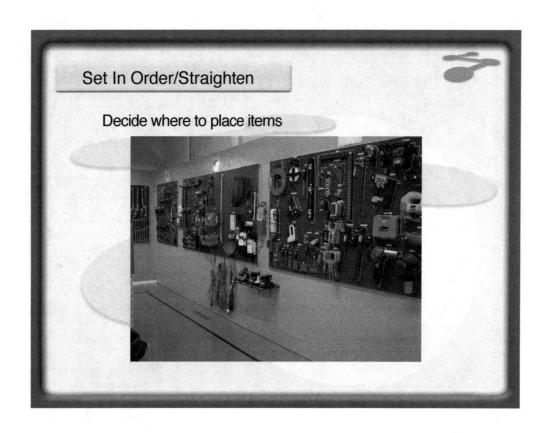

Notes, Slide 25:

_____

_____

_____

_____

_____

_____

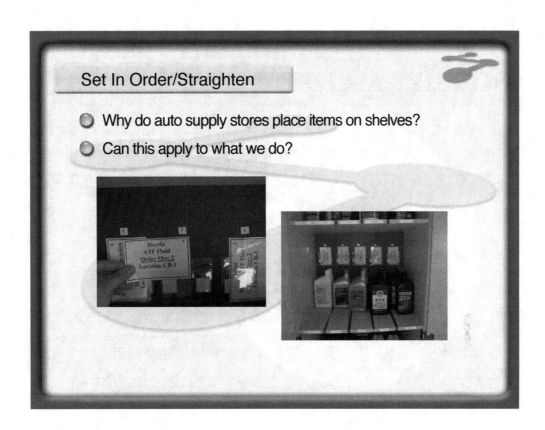

Notes, Slide 26:

_____

_____

_____

_____

_____

_____

Tip:
Try to reach for anything in your work area. The goal of Set In Order is to eliminate reaching.

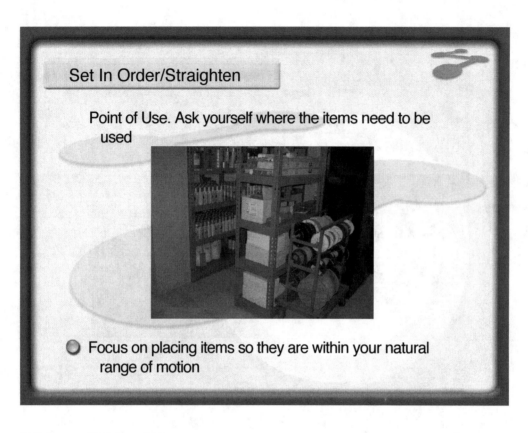

Notes, Slide 27:

_____

_____

_____

_____

_____

_____

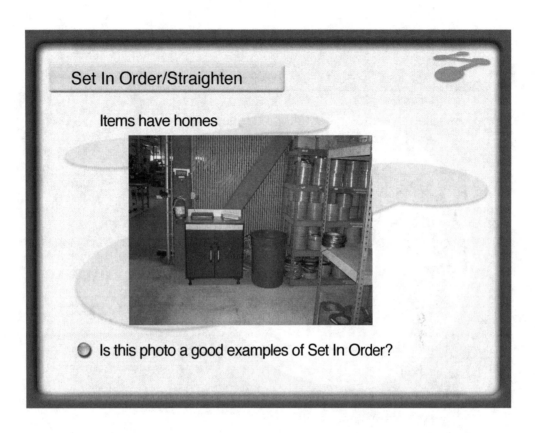

Set In Order/Straighten

Items have homes

Is this photo a good examples of Set In Order?

Notes, Slide 28:

Tip:
Use Set In Order to get working, rather than just preparing to work.

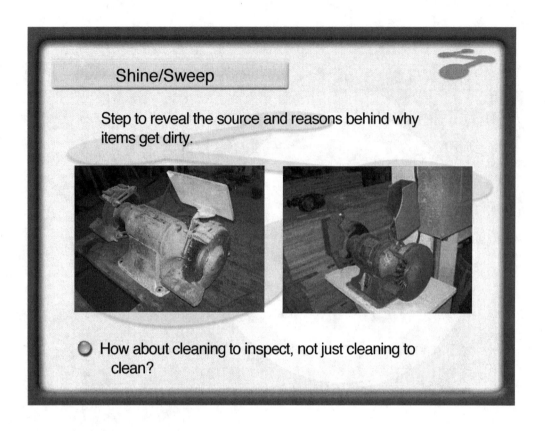

Shine/Sweep

Step to reveal the source and reasons behind why items get dirty.

How about cleaning to inspect, not just cleaning to clean?

Notes, Slide 29:

_____

_____

_____

_____

Shine Action Defined: _____

_____

Additional Example: _____

_____

Tip:
Remember, we are cleaning to...

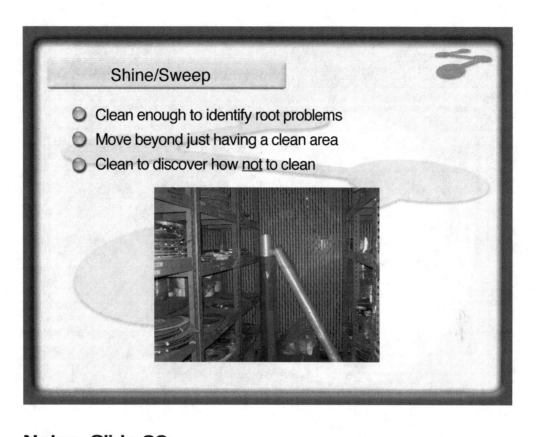

Notes, Slide 30:

_____

_____

_____

_____

_____

_____

Additional Example: _____

_____

Question:

Why are we cleaning during this workshop?

_____

_____

_____

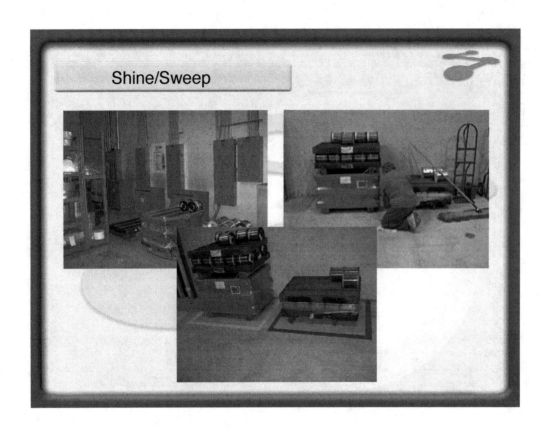

Notes, Slide 31:

_____

_____

_____

_____

_____

Tip:
Combining ideas together will find solutions to reducing and even eliminating the need for shining.

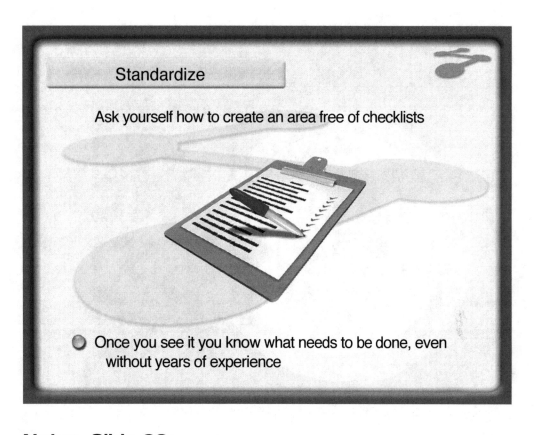

Notes, Slide 32:

_____

_____

_____

_____

_____

_____

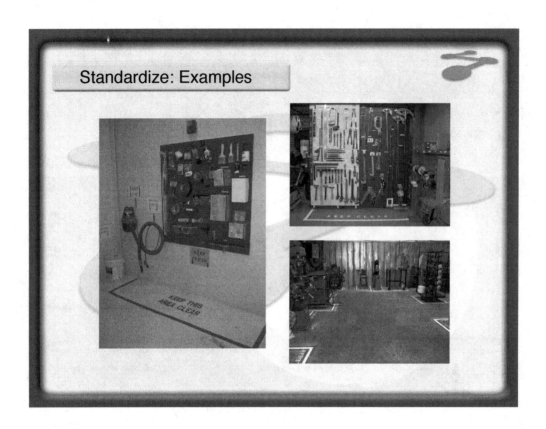

Notes, Slide 33:

_____

_____

_____

_____

Standardize Action Defined: _____

_____

Additional Example: _____

Tip:
When creating a standard, incorporate a symbol, color, and/or physical characteristics.

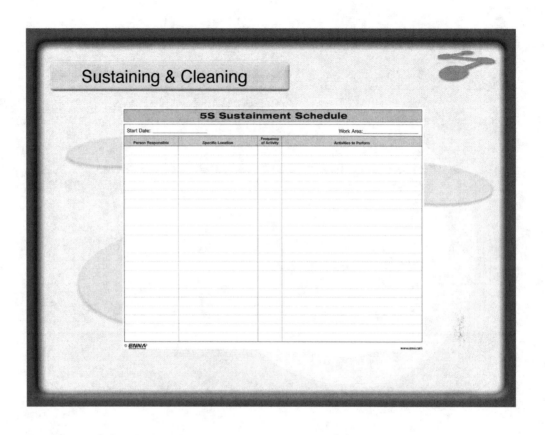

Notes, Slide 34:

_____

_____

_____

_____

_____

_____

Question:

Why is it useful to employ the 5S Sustainment Schedule?

_____

_____

_____

Sustain

- Keep asking how to simplify the issue in order to sustain

- The idea: if we have less self-discipline, it will be easier to sustain

Notes, Slide 35:

_____

_____

_____

_____

_____

_____

Question:

What is the ultimate goal of 5S?

_____

_____

_____

Sustain

- Management shows commitment to program
- Everyone leads by being an example of 5S
- 5S is a component to every shop
- Goal is to have business customers be able to tour your facility
- Use the Auditing 5S Forms to assess 5S score

Notes, Slide 36:

_____

_____

_____

_____

Sustain Action Defined: _____

_____

Additional Example: _____

_____

Tip:
Use your past employment experience to help develop sustaining changes. Often past examples help develop solutions. Pull examples from the past and see how the team can use them.

Notes, Slide 37:

_____

_____

_____

_____

_____

_____

Long Term 5S Success

- Management is expected to be involved
- Involvement of everyone
- 8 Wastes are an integral part of 5S
- Link improvement to financial benefit

Notes, Slide 38:

_____

_____

_____

_____

_____

_____

Question:

5S needs the commitment of who?

_____

_____

_____

Review

- What are the 5S's?
- Which "S" is the most important?
- Can you relate to the need for 5S?
- What are the 8 Wastes?
- What is your responsibility?

Notes, Slide 39:

_____

_____

_____

_____

Final thoughts on this section: _____

_____

_____

Tip:
Write down the answers to these questions to summarize this section.

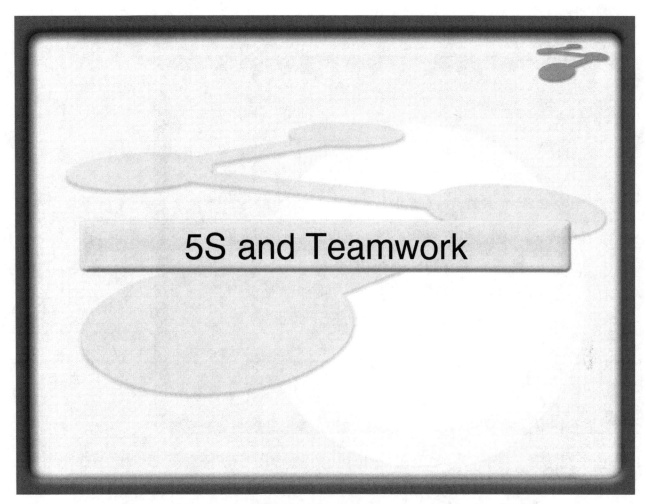

5S and Teamwork

Participant Workbook

In this Section

- Transform knowledge into practice
- Learn the 5S Auditing Process
- Learn the 30 Day Action Log
- Learn the 5S Sustainment Schedule
- Discuss the workshop format in the specific work areas

It is time to start putting the 5S principles into practice, and the first step is to form discussions and demonstrations around the worksheets that we will be using, which is the final picture culminating in the 5S Board. We will teach the idea of going through the areas the first time in order to get a baseline, then we can see where the biggest opportunities are regarding 5S. There will be small teams working together as they assess and collect information to form an action plan for the rest of the work area.

 Suggestion   **Tip**   **Question**

5S Teamwork

Steps:

1: 5S Audit

2: Sort - Red Tag Activity

3: Set In Order/Straighten - Point of Use Storage

4: Shine/Sweep - Clean Area

5: Standardize - Visual Management

6: Sustain - Refine and Schedule

Notes, Slide 41:

_____

_____

_____

_____

_____

_____

5S Team

Initial Audit

1. Auditing 5S Team (2-3 People)

2. Photography Team (2 People)
   - Take pictures of the current state
   - Highlight key items and areas

3. 5S Mapping Team (2-3 People)
   - Layout where vehicles, people, supplies, and equipment should be located (bird's eye view)

Notes, Slide 42:

_____

_____

Team Assigned To: _____

_____

Team Members Names: _____

_____

_____

Assigned Work Area:

_____

Additional Information: _____

_____

_____

Tip:
You will change roles as you move from assessment through to making changes, but your team should stay together.

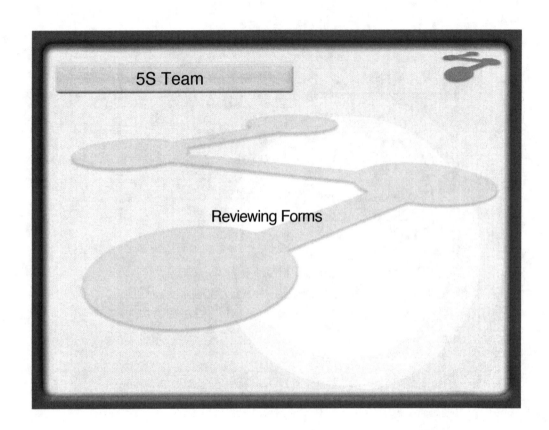

5S Team

Reviewing Forms

5S Mapping

Notes, Slide 44:

_____

_____

_____

_____

_____

_____

5S Evaluation Review

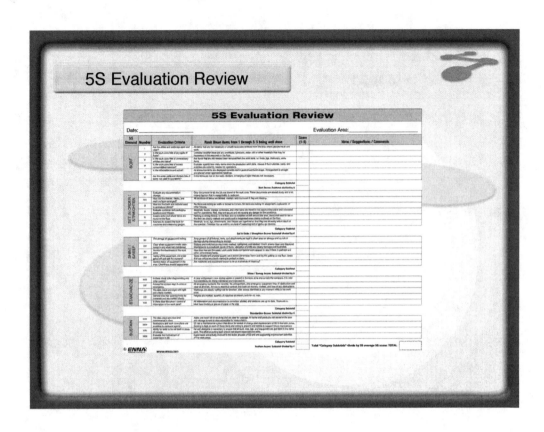

Notes, Slide 45:

_____

_____

_____

_____

_____

Tip:
Be critical when evaluating the area; the initial evaluation serves as a baseline for further comparison.

Photos

Good
Lighting

Bad
Lighting

Notes, Slide 46:

Tip:

Lighting is key for photographs. Have the team borrow lights to make the items in the pictures really stand out.

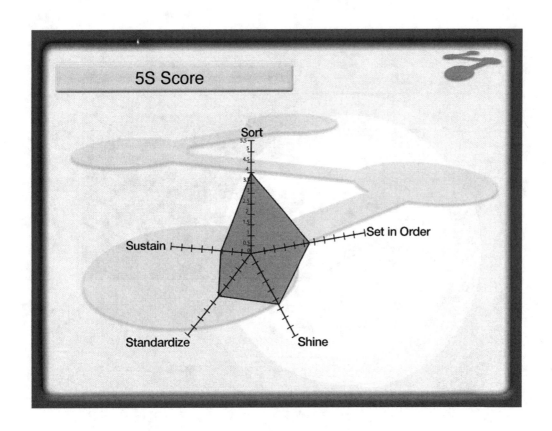

Notes, Slide 47:

_____

_____

_____

_____

_____

_____

Tip:
We should be ready to evaluate our current state.

Notes, Slide 48 & 49:

Tip:

If you have any doubt, Red Tag it and "throw it out" of the area.

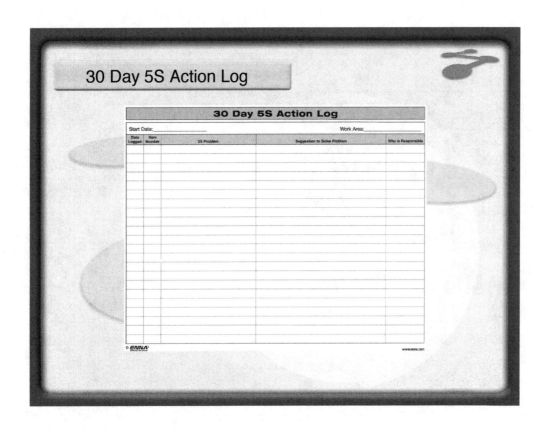

30 Day 5S Action Log

Notes, Slide 50:

Tip:
Only place items on the 30 Day 5S Action Log that the team has agreed is an item for that list. Your team should all agree before adding an item to the 30 Day 5S Action Log. You may have to get support from other departments.

Notes, Slide 51:

_____

_____

_____

_____

_____

_____

Tip:

Team members are expected to commit to 5S by providing innovative ways to solve problems.

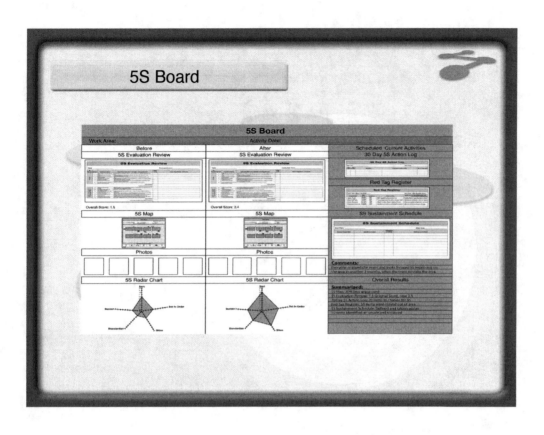

Notes, Slide 52:

_____

_____

_____

_____

_____

_____

5S Supply Chain & Logistics Assessment

Facilitator: _____ Name: _____

Workshop: _____ Date: _____

Circle or write the answer that best fits the question or completes the statement.

1. _____ 5S originally had _____ S's.
   a) 4
   b) 1
   c) 2

2. _____ What company started what is now known as 5S?
   a) Volvo
   b) Toyota
   c) Ford

3. _____ What is the first S of the 5S's?
   a) Set In Order/Straighten
   b) Sort
   c) Shine

4. _____ Of the 8 Wastes of Supply Chain & Logistics, which one is the worst?
   a) Overproduction
   b) Inventory
   c) Motion

5. _____ If a company implements 5S successfully, the need for self discipline is _____.
   a) Eliminated
   b) Reduced
   c) Increased

6. _____ 5S is one of the building blocks of _____.
   a) Operations
   b) Cleanliness
   c) Lean

7. _____ Why do we clean during 5S?
   a) To inspect
   b) Because it is the right thing to do
   c) To prevent bad parts

8. _____ Inventory exists as _____.
   a) Raw, WIP, FG
   b) GF, WIP, RAW
   c) PIW, WAR, FG

9. _____ The 2nd S, Set In Order/Straighten, allows for a person to have minimal _____.
   a) Work
   b) Waiting
   c) Motion

10. _____ What is the 5S Sustainment Schedule used for?
    a) Recording workshop activity
    b) Recording the cleaning that is needed
    c) Scheduling the next workshop

11. _____ For 5S to be successful we need the involvement of _____.
    a) Top management
    b) Entire department
    c) Everyone

12. _____ The 5S Map provides a simple _____ view of the work area.
    a) Bird's eye
    b) Planning
    c) Outline

13. _____ Extra Processing is the hardest waste to find because _____.
    a) There are so many processes
    b) It may initially seem to be a Value-Added step
    c) It is totally necessary

14. _____ The 30-Day Action Log allows the company to _____.
    a) Document a list of unsolvable problems
    b) List workshop problems to be solved on one document
    c) Demonstrate its commitment to 5S

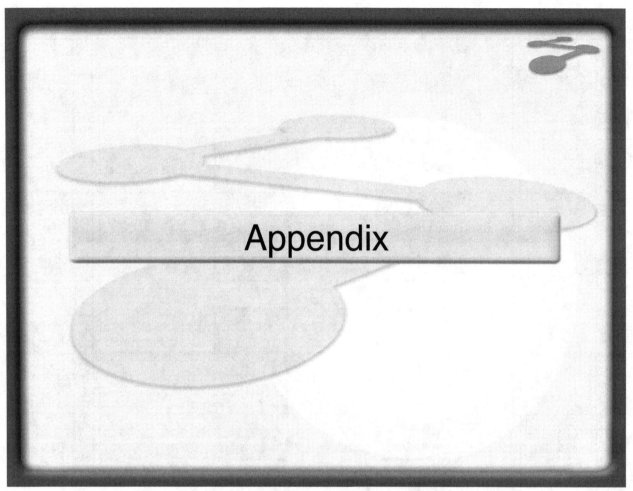

Appendix

Participant Workbook

In this Section

You will find copies of the forms used in the workshop filled out for your reference.

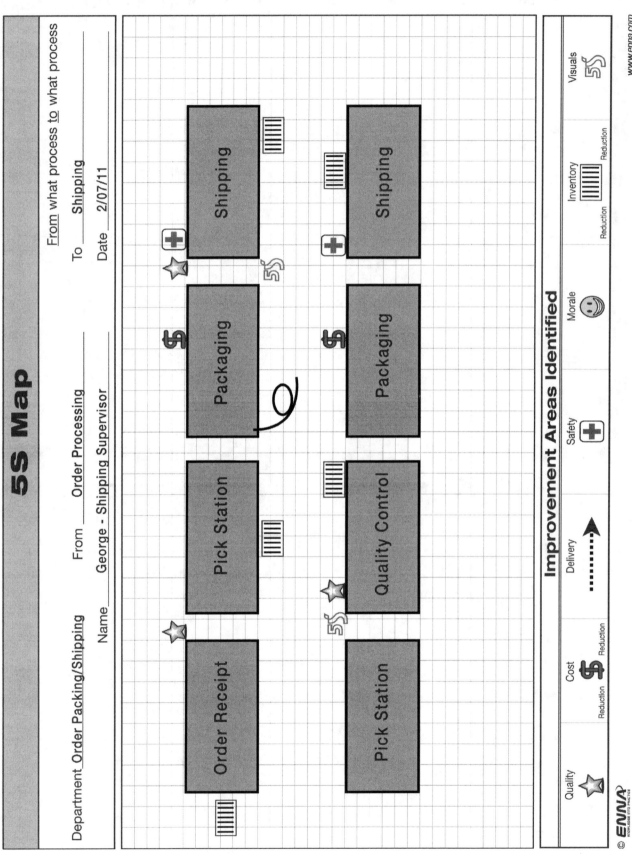

5S Map

Department Order Packing/Shipping

From _____ Order Processing _____ To _____ Shipping _____

From what process to what process

Name _____ George - Shipping Supervisor _____ Date _____ 2/07/11 _____

Order Receipt

Pick Station

Packaging

Shipping

Pick Station

Quality Control

Packaging

Shipping

Improvement Areas Identified

Quality	Cost	Delivery	Safety	Morale	Inventory	Visuals
	Reduction				Reduction Reduction	

www.enna.com

5S Evaluation Review

Date: _____   Evaluation Area: _____

5S Element	Number	Evaluation Criteria	Rank these items from 1 through 5: 5 being well done	Score (1-5)	Ideas / Suggestions / Comments
SORT	I	Are the aisles and walkways open and clear?	All items that are not necessary or unsafe have been removed from the area where people travel and work.		
	II	Is the work zone free of any spills of fluids?	Consider whether there are any chemicals, lubricants, water, oils or other materials that may be hazardous in the area and on the floor.		
	III	Is the work zone free of unnecessary articles and items?	Are items that are not needed been removed from the work zone. i.e. tools, jigs, stationary, extra items.		
	IV	Is the work zone free of excess consumables/materials?	Evaluate against how many items are in the production work zone. Assess if the materials, parts, and supplies are currently needed for operations.		
	V	Is the information board active?	All announcements are displayed currently and in good presentable shape. Arrangement is straight and placed under appropriate headings.		
	VI	Are the areas walls and dividers free of items not used in operations?	Extra items are not on the walls, dividers, or hanging of signs that are not necessary.		
			Sort Score: Subtotal divided by 6	**Category Subtotal**	
SET IN ORDER / STRAIGHTEN	VII	Evaluate any documentation storage.	Only documents to do the job are stored at the work zone. These documents are stored nicely and in an orderly fashion that is recognizable to outsiders.		
	VIII	How are the shelves, desks, and work surfaces arranged?	All locations of items are labelled, marked, and it is known if they are missing.		
	IX	How are the tools and material used in operations stored?	No items are resting on walls or tucked in corners. No items are resting on equipment, cupboards, or other fixtures.		
	X	Evaluate container and packaging locations and tidiness.	Materials, boxes, storage containers, and other items are stored in the appropriate place and orientated well for operations. Also, they are secure and not causing any danger to the workforce.		
	XI	Assess order and where items are found on the floor.	Nothing is sitting directly on the floor and no materials are left around the area. Items that need to be on the floor are clearly marked and positioned in designated areas clearly outlined on the floor.		
	XII	Easiness to access the tools for machines and measuring gauges.	Materials, tools, jigs, attachments, and fixtures are organized so that they are all easily within reach of the operator. Consider this as well for any kind of measuring tool or go/no-go devices.		
			Set in Order / Straighten Score: Subtotal divided by 6	**Category Subtotal**	
SHINE / SWEEP	XIII	The storage of gauges and tooling.	Arrangement of all fixtures, tools, and attachments are kept in clean area for storage and no risk of damage during transporting to storage.		
	XIV	Clear when equipment needs maintenance and when last maintained.	Buttons and switches on machinery marked, highlighted, and labeled. Check sheets clean and displayed. Maintenance is scheduled; levels of fluids, lubrication of joints are clearly itemized and illustrated.		
	XV	Assess the cleanliness of the work zone.	How dust free are the areas. Look under desks and behind work spaces to see if there is garbage and other unnecessary items.		
	XVI	Safety of the equipment, are areas gated off and safe for workers?	Spray shields and physical guards are in active use to keep items and liquids getting on the floor. Areas that are critical are clearly marked to protect workers.		
	XVII	Assess status of equipment in the area. Cleanliness overall appearance.	Are machines and equipment known to be on a schedule of cleaning?		
			Shine / Sweep Score: Subtotal divided by 5	**Category Subtotal**	
STANDARDIZE	XVIII	Is there visual color diagramming and color coding?	A clear and present color coding system is present in the work zone and across the company. It is clear that standards are being maintained and improved on.		
	XIX	Assess the access ways in case of emergency.	All emergency systems; fire vehicles, fire extinguishers, and emergency equipment free of obstruction and clear at all times. Access to electrical controls and fuses are known, marked, and free of any obstructions.		
	XX	The aisle ways are bright with light and clearly marked.	Walkways are clearly highlighted for direction, aisle access identified at any moment while in the work zone.		
	XXI	General area has quantity limits for materials and are marked clearly.	Heights are marked, quantity of materials are known, and min vs. max.		
	XXII	Is there clear document control of information in the work zone?	All information and documentation is controlled, labeled, and revisions are up to date. There are no label-less binders or pieces of paper in the area.		
			Standardize Score: Subtotal divided by 5	**Category Subtotal**	
SUSTAIN	XXIII	The aisle ways are clean and maintenance is clear.	Aisles are never full of anything and are clear for passage. All items and products not stored in the aisle and storage is next to aisle accessible for transportation.		
	XXIV	Illustrations and work zone plans are available to compare against.	5S has a maintenance system that allows for control of change and improvement of 5S in the work zones. Scoring is kept on each of these items and history is present and visible to support future improvement.		
	XXV	Ability for tools to be set back in place of storage.	No self-discipline is necessary to ensure that all tools, dies, jigs, and equipment are put back in the same spot. The effort of putting back should not require organizational skills.		
	XXVI	Evaluate the involvement of supervisors in 5S.	Supervisors are actively involved in the review process of 5S and are supporting improvement activities of the work areas.		
			Sustain Score: Subtotal divided by 4	**Category Subtotal**	

Total "Category Subtotals" divide by 26 average 5S score: TOTAL

© ENNA   www.enna.com

Red Tag Register

Project Date: __April 7-10, 2011__

Work Area: __Order Packaging__

Item Description	Date Sorted	Log Number	Reason for Tag	Classification (i.e. need approval, other dept. needs to assess, throw out, etc.)
Tape Machine	4/7/11	001	Old and Not Functioning	Try to Fix if not fixable then throw out.
Assorted Tools	4/8/11	002	Too complicated to select proper tool.	Maintenance will decide - throw or repair.
Extra Material	4/9/11	003	Need to clear floor & desk of items.	Thrown away by Packing Mngr - no value.

30 Day 5S Action Log

Start Date: __2/10/2011__

Work Area: __Order Picking__

Date Logged	Item Number	5S Problem	Suggestion to Solve Problem	Who is Responsible
2/15/10	1	Pick Carts difficult to maneuver	Put carts on different casters for ease of movement	Jared F.
2/17/10	2	Pick Carts in the way	Create designated "Pick Cart Storage Area"	Henry S.
2/20/10	3	Pull Orders in no particular order	Pull Order paperwork system - In Progress, FIFO, etc.	Troy G.
2/20/10	4	Pens constantly disappearing	Create a pen holder for Pick Carts so pens are available	Jan T.

5S Sustainment Schedule

Start Date: _April 08, 2011_

Work Area: _Packing_

Person Responsible	Specific Location	Frequency of Activity	Activities to Perform
Sue Johannasen	Final Packaging Assembly	daily	Clean up workbench that holds packing material and tape.